KICKING OFF

GETTING STARTED IN THE CHRISTIAN LIFE

by

Alan Stewart
and
Edward Vaughan

ST MATTHIAS PRESS

© St Matthias Press, 1992

St Matthias Press Ltd (A.C.N. 067 558 365)
PO Box 225
KINGSFORD NSW 2032
Ph (02) 663 1478 Fax (02) 662 4289

ISBN 1 875245 22 7

Typesetting and design by St Matthias Press
Printed in Australia by Openbook Publishers

To our wives,
Kathy and Jane

KICKING OFF

GETTING STARTED
IN THE CHRISTIAN LIFE

CONTENTS

CONTENTS

KICKING OFF

Welcome—to this book and to the kingdom of God! For if you're reading this book, we assume that you have recently decided to become a Christian. It's great to have you in the family.

In the pages that follow you'll find a variety of things designed to help you as you kick off in the Christian life:

- you'll eavesdrop on letters written to Dave, a young Christian
- you'll read stories about real people who've become Christians, and who look back at the lessons they've learnt
- you'll be given practical tips on things like praying and reading the Bible
- you'll read case studies on some of the nuts and bolts issues of Christian living (like how to handle money or how to deal with sex).

All in all, this book aims to tell you the basic things that you need to know to get started as a Christian. We haven't covered everything—far from it—but we've tried to convey the essential things.

Kicking Off is designed to work in tandem with *Just for Starters*, a set of seven basic Bible studies, also published by St Matthias Press. If you're doing these studies with someone, you'll find that the book fits in well with what you're studying week by week. We'd recommend that you try to do these studies with an older (that is, more mature) Christian sometime soon. If that's not possible, you could perhaps do the studies by yourself, using this book to help you along. If even that is not possible, don't despair—the book stands quite well on its own.

We pray that as you read, God will teach you about himself and about how you can live as his son or daughter.

Now it's time to meet Dave and his friend, Michael.

DEAR DAVE

Your letter was one of the sneakiest that I have ever read. You told me about work, about the movie you had seen and the party that you had been to. And then right at the end you slipped in a little comment about our previous conversations. A faltering, hesitant, intriguing little comment: "I've been thinking seriously about what you've been telling me about Jesus and I prayed the prayer. What's the next step?"

Dave, this is the absolute best news in the entire world! It should be shouted from the rooftops and shown on prime time television. Instead you hide it at the end of your letter!

As you kick off the Christian life, I'd like to mention a few things so that you understand what you are doing. Before I was a Christian, I thought it was all about obeying a lot of rules that were carefully designed to make life miserable, or at least terminally boring. It wasn't until after God had dragged me into his kingdom that I realized that being a Christian is about knowing and loving a person. So let me tell you what kind of a person Jesus is.

Jesus says that he came so that people might have life and have it to the full. Life might not be easier or trouble free for you now, but I guarantee that if you get serious about following Jesus you will suck the marrow out of life.

What's so special about Jesus? Well, how long have you got? The Bible tells us that Jesus is fully and truly human and at the same time fully and truly God. The God who made this universe is so big that we find him hard to understand, but he became a human being so that we could know what he is like. We talk about it every Christmas, but we don't often stop to think that God became a baby, was born in a shed and slept in a feed-box. If we'd been born at the right time and the right place, we could have sat down, shared a meal with him and listened to him explain about his Father.

While Jesus lived among us he did things that only God can do. He healed the sick, raised the dead and fed crowds of thousands from one lunchbox. (You can find all these stories in the New Testament.) He also forgave the sins people had committed against God.

Jesus showed us God's power and compassion in action when his friend Lazarus died. Lazarus had been dead for four days when Jesus arrived at his tomb. And Jesus wept. Then, after he had prayed to his Father, Jesus called to Lazarus and the dead man walked out of the tomb, much to the crowd's amazement!

People were also amazed at the way Jesus spoke, because he had an authority which came from God. Even people who hated Jesus admitted that there was something special about the way he taught. The Jewish religious leaders once sent some guards to arrest Jesus. When they turned up, Jesus was teaching. They arrived back empty-handed and, when their bosses asked them to explain why, the guards answered: "No-one ever spoke the way this man does". As I read today what Jesus taught, I am absolutely convinced they are the very words of God.

But the thing that really stands out is the purpose of Jesus' life. In Mark 10:45, Jesus says that he came not to be served by people, but to serve people and to give his life as a ransom for our sins. Jesus came for the express purpose of dying in our place—taking the punishment for our sinfulness. The Son of God—all powerful and perfect—left his Father and came to live in our lowly world and to die so that we could be forgiven our sins.

This is real love—love that will change our lives when we understand it. Jesus said to his friends on the night before he died, "No one has greater love than this, that a man would lay down his life for his friends". Jesus was a one-man rescue mission, to save us from hell and win for us the gift of eternal life.

Dave, what really hits me is that Jesus didn't just die for the great sea of humanity; he died for me. And this is something that I never grow tired of thinking about. It will fill you with wonder for the rest of your Christian life. Jesus gave his life for us. And all we have to do is trust him. Amazing.

The Christian life is about knowing and trusting Jesus. The way you get to know him better is to read about him in the New Testament, and Mark's Gospel is a good book to start with. There's a million other things I want to tell you, but that will do for now. I'm so happy that you've kicked off the Christian life. You'll be hearing from me soon.

Love,

Michael

CHAPTER 1

SAVED BY GOD

DEAR DAVE

I am still rejoicing with you (along with the angels in heaven, I might add!) at the magnificent news that you have become a Christian. Believe me, there is nothing more exciting or important in life than to see someone make that decision. And I'm sure that you are beginning to realize the greatness of the changes that have taken place in your life. In the truest sense of the word, they are cosmic.

I know that your knowledge of the Bible is not vast, and I understand that you are still coming to terms with the fact that things are different between you and God. Because of this, I thought that I would share with you a Bible passage which helped me a lot when I was still a nipper-Christian like yourself.

Romans 5:6-8 is the passage. (Have you worked out how to look things up in the Bible yet? It took me ages!) Just to help you, I'll write it out:

> You see, at just the right time, when we were still powerless, Christ died for the ungodly. Very rarely will anyone die for a righteous man, though for a good man someone might possibly dare to die. But God demonstrates his own love for us in this: While we were still sinners, Christ died for us.

What does it all mean? Think about it like this. What has your life been like up to this point? You haven't been spectacularly bad by human standards. No murder, no rape, no pillage.

Some fairly low grade sex, drugs and rock and roll. That makes you just about average in Australian terms. But seen from God's point of view, you have been a rebel. For a long time you knew what God wanted from you, but you made a deliberate choice to to turn away from him. You told God to make himself scarce, because you wanted to decide for yourself what was right and wrong in your life.

Now this makes you a rebel (just like the rest of humanity, by the way). A rebel who faces punishment. God has every right to obliterate you, because you were deliberately defying him. That's the bad news. It's what the Bible calls judgement.

And the bad news gets worse. There is absolutely no reason why God should do anything to help you. Why should he save you from hell? It's only what you deserve, after all. You've been telling him to get lost for some time now, and God would be perfectly justified to simply say, "You don't want anything to do with me, so I'll respect your decision. You will go to a place where you will exist without me and without all the good things I have given you. You will go to hell."

If you had a best mate whom you loved, would you die for him if he were in danger? Well you might—you just might, if you were courageous and he was a very good friend. But what about someone who was your enemy, who ignored you or, even worse, insulted and despised you when you were kind to him? What would you do for him if he was in danger?

My guess is that you are the same as most other people— you would dance on his grave. Well my friend, that just shows the difference between us and God. At the time when we hated God, God didn't show us anger; he showed us love. God has not punished you and me as we deserve, because his Son Jesus volunteered to take that punishment instead. That is why

Jesus' death on the cross is the absolute centre of what it means to be a Christian. We believe that when Jesus died on the cross, he died as an innocent man in the place of the guilty—you, me and everyone else.

Now the Bible has a number of different ways of describing this. It uses many different expressions to help us understand the enormity of what Jesus has done. Let me explain some of these briefly:

We have been *justified*. Justification is a legal term. You see, we have all broken the law of God, and because of that we stand before him as guilty. We deserve punishment. But Jesus has taken that punishment for us by dying on the cross. When he died, he received the penalty that was due to us. Because of what Jesus has done, God the Judge can now declare us acquitted—the case against us is closed. This is what it means to be 'justified'. The people who trust in Jesus are now called 'righteous' by God; that is, right with him.

We have been given *new life*. Once upon a time we were like dead people because of our sins. But now that our sins are forgiven, we have a new life. We are new people because of Christ's death for us. It is not because of anything we have or haven't done; it is a gift from God. And once you have been reborn, you stay that way!

We have been *adopted*. We have become part of God's family. Jesus is God's Son and, by bringing us into a relationship with God, Jesus has given us a new and special status before God. Now we can call God 'Father', because there is a close personal relationship between us, just like in a human family. In 2 Corinthians 6:18, Paul calls us God's sons and daughters. It means we have a special relationship with God and with other

Christian believers.

We have been *sanctified*. This word means 'made holy' or 'dedicated to God'. God now sees us as clean and holy because of Jesus' death. And he is turning us into the kind of people that we should be (I take it that you've noticed that you haven't become perfect overnight). We will spend the rest of our lives asking God to make us the people that we should be.

Each of these words explains a different aspect of Jesus' death for us. There are also other words, but coming to terms with the ones I've mentioned will keep you busy enough. We have been declared absolutely innocent, not because of anything that we have done, but because of what Jesus has done. Now it's important to get this right at the very beginning. If you don't, you will very quickly find yourself led astray. Let me point out an example.

At the moment, I suspect you feel excited about being a Christian. There is a sense of newness and adventure about it. The bad news is that the feeling won't last. Some people never feel at all different when they become Christians. The fact is that emotions are an unreliable guide in this area.

Some people question the reality of their faith, especially after having committed some sin that they consider especially shocking. I remember soon after I became a Christian, waking up after a night of liquid indulgence with my partners-in-crime. Apart from the hangover and the shame, I was convinced that I was no longer a Christian—how could I be? The things I had done were in no way consistent with my faith in Christ.

What do you do when you aren't sure of your salvation? Don't look at the way you feel inside yourself. You won't find the answer there. Look at Jesus on the cross. Then ask yourself the question, "Does God love me?". And the answer is absolutely definitely completely YES. Jesus chose to die for me—that's how I know how much he loves me.

Dave, I've been a Christian for over a decade now and I never stop coming back to one fact—Christ died for me. The more I understand about the Christian life, the more I understand that Jesus' death on the cross is what it's all about.

One last thing before I go. When you do the wrong thing again (as you probably will), talk to God and say "I'm sorry; please forgive me because of what Jesus has done. Help me not to do it again." It's what the Bible calls repentance. Repentance is more than feeling sorry; it's changing how you live. It's a handy concept to understand. You'll be using it more than once before your life on earth is over, I promise you.

Love,

Michael

T   R   U   E   S   T   O   R   I   E   S

JOHN
AGE: 37

"This may sound obvious, but the thing new Christians have to keep central is Christ. You don't need to know everything straight away; you'll work things out in time. But you mustn't lose sight of the cross."

For John, becoming a Christian was a little like coming home. He'd been to Sunday School and youth group as a kid—he was even roped into being the church organist for a while. But during that time, he had not known God and was looking for an excuse to get out. It was 15 years later, when he was in his mid-30s, that his attitude started to change.

"The thing that really started to change everything was the death of my father four years ago. We were very close. It all sat very uncomfortably with me. I wasn't sure whether he was a Christian or not, although he was a good man. You get that gnawing feeling: what happens to you when you die? What happened to my father?

"Just at that time, we employed an engineer at work who was also working part-time for her church. It struck me that she was different. I asked her a few questions and started reading my Bible again. As it happened, we were talking about her church and it turned out that the person who was preaching the following Sunday had preached at my old church 15 years ago. So I turned up to hear him. We remembered one another, and he offered to do some private Bible study with me, and I subsequently decided to become a Christian. That was just over 12 months ago."

Becoming a Christian changed a lot of things for John, including his relationships with his friends. This has been the hardest thing for him so far.

"A lot of my friends are avoiding the issue. They've known me for a long time, some of them, and I get the feeling that they're dying to know why I've done what I've done—but they aren't game to ask yet. It's going to come, and fairly soon I think. Waiting for that time to come is hard. Some of my friends are going to accept my decision to become a Christian for what it is; I know that there are one or two who won't, and it will probably damage those relationships irreparably. These are people I've known for 25 years. I have a bit of fear about that.

"On the other hand, it may present an opportunity. I think that the people whom I expect to react worst are the people who are least comfortable with their own situation. They'll want to know 'why?' the most."

And what has been the best thing about becoming a Christian?

"It has changed my attitude to relationships; I think of things differently, and no matter how difficult things are, the internal turmoil that I was feeling before has been resolved. I don't have that any more. I always think of that 'peace which passes all understanding'—it's a great relief not to have that battle, where you're fighting God every day."

Like most Christians, John struggles with a certain degree of chaos in his Bible reading and prayer times, as well as with periods of doubt.

"The best description of my prayer and Bible reading at the moment is that it is a little haphazard, but I'm becoming more disciplined—although I've got this suspicion that I might still be saying that in 10 years time. I keep coming back to the book of Romans, which was the first book I started to read when I took up the Bible again. I find it a compelling book, and I'm still tackling it. It's been a project for nearly 15 months now! Prayer is something we're getting better organized with as a family, praying with the children and so on.

"Another struggle is that every now and then, a huge amount of uncertainty can descend on you. You're standing in church singing a hymn and you suddenly think, 'Why am I here?'. I have these flashes of uncertainty every now and then, and it's as if the intellectual understanding of what you've done and why just deserts you for a moment."

And what advice would John give a new Christian?

"This may sound obvious, but the thing new Christians have to keep central is Christ. It is so very easy when you first become a Christian to get bogged down in intellectualizing and a whole lot of other peripheral things. You want to get things straight in your mind and work out exactly what and why you believe. And that's fair enough, but you can put the cross of Christ to one side. You have to keep thinking about the cross and what happened there for you. You don't need to know everything straight away; you'll work things out in time. But you mustn't lose sight of the cross. Keep thinking and praying about that, and the other things will fall into place."

CHAPTER 2

TRUSTING IN GOD

KICKING OFF

DEAR DAVE

Yesterday my boss gave me a motivational tape. (What's he trying to tell me?) As I was listening to it in the car, I was struck by the fact that part of the speaker's message was similar to the Bible. He was talking about leaders being servants, that good managers are those who have found the true purpose of their life. As far as I could tell, the speaker wasn't a Christian, but there was much that I agreed with.

Except for one thing. He was basically saying that what counts is what you achieve; that the more you do the more you will impress. Now that's not a controversial message—I think it's what the non-Christian world tells us all the time. But it's not what the Bible tells us, and it's not the way that God relates to us. In fact, this is the single biggest mistake that people make when they think about God. They believe that God will love them if they are good and he will not love them if they are bad. The message of the Bible is completely different.

Think about this verse in the Bible. Ephesians 2:8-9 says:

> For it is by grace you have been saved, through faith—and this not from yourselves, it is the gift of God—not by works, so that no-one can boast.

Paul's message here is absolutely revolutionary. Most Australians reckon they understand Christianity, but if they knew what Paul was really saying, they would be stunned (and probably become Christians themselves!). Paul's message is: bad people go to heaven.

Remember I mentioned in my last letter that we were all rebels, that we were God's enemies? We were in no position to save ourselves. We were totally cactus and we needed someone to save us.

My friend Simon was walking along a beach one day when he saw a guy face down in shallow water. There was a crowd of people on the sand just looking on. It appeared to Simon that the man was drowning, but he thought perhaps he was just swimming. But he stopped and looked. Something about the man's loose limbs and his aimless floating convinced him that the guy wasn't swimming—he *was* drowning. Simon bolted down and dragged the guy out. Fortunately, Simon knew mouth to mouth resuscitation and the guy was saved. Apparently, he'd been surfing, had fallen off his board and was knocked unconscious in the shallow water. In another couple of minutes he would've been dead.

Incredible, isn't it—drowning in shallow water with dozens of people looking on. Well, our situation is similar. We were drowning and couldn't save ourselves, but Jesus acted like a lifesaver and rescued us. What did we contribute to the whole exercise? Nothing! We were simply the mugs who were drowning. And we were lucky that the right person came along to help us at just the right time.

How does a rescued person feel? Somewhat embarrassed I suspect. None of us like the feeling of being dependent upon other people. But the rescued person also feels grateful, in spite of that. Without help, he would have been dead. It's nothing to boast about—how could it be? All he did was allow some hero to save him. The best he can do is to say 'thanks'.

You see the parallel? We were hopeless sinners, unable to save ourselves, ruining our lives and heading for hell. Jesus rescued us. What did we contribute? Our sin, our helplessness and nothing else. So I can't really boast about being saved—all I can do is thank God. Being saved is *totally* a gift from God.

Dave, let me make this as clear as I can. When I'm talking about being sinful, I'm talking about our attitude toward God. Human beings love being independent from God, and hate the idea that we need to depend on him. And that is the heart of sin. Sin is saying, "I want to be the boss of my life; God can stay out".

Some people who try to be independent of God (i.e. sinners) appear like nice, charming, happy people. Some are anti-social thugs. But from God's point of view they are all telling him to get lost—and it's still sin either way.

Do you ever wonder whether you are good enough to be a Christian? Well, you're not. Salvation is a gift from God. You didn't earn it. You never could earn it. He didn't owe it to you. It was a freebie, like someone walking up to you on the street and putting $100 in your hand—absolutely free.

Should you be boastful or proud about the fact that you've been saved? Of course not. You didn't achieve anything. You simply received a gift. The special one is the one who gave the gift.

What should your response be to God's generous gift? You should be thankful. You should do the things that please Jesus and I don't only mean helping little old ladies across the road. I mean showing your gratitude by the way you live all of your life all of the time—the way that you drive, the way you spend money, the way you use your time—these are all opportunities to express your thanks to Jesus.

Let me give you one example. Once upon a time, you spent all the money that you earned on yourself, trying to satisfy your own desires. If you wanted it, and you thought it was going to make you happy, you went out and bought it. But now you have been saved. You are so thankful to Jesus that you want to see other people saved too. So you cheerfully give money to support people whose job is to tell people about Jesus and help them become Christians. That is a good thing to do, a grateful response to God. You don't do it to win brownie points; you do it because it pleases your heavenly Father who has been so kind to you already.

Imagine a train. It's made up of an engine and some carriages. If it's going to work properly then you've got to get them in the right order—the engine first followed by the carriages. Well, what we're talking about is the same. First comes being saved by Jesus' death on the cross. Then comes the good things that you do as a result of your new life. That is the correct order. If you reverse them, it doesn't work. You can't do good things which please God *before* you are a Christian.

Jesus only saves bad people, the ones who admit they have done wrong and need to be saved. And that is real love. Take care,

Love,

Michael

GEORGIE

AGE: 29

"Accepting that Jesus actually died for me and that I was special enough and worthwhile enough for Jesus to do such a tragic thing for me was the hardest thing."

When Georgie decided to have her daughter baptized, she didn't realize that her whole life was about to change. She did a six-week 'Christianity Explained' course with her local minister and, by the end of it, had become a Christian. She found it hard to believe that God had shown his love for her in such a sacrificial way: "Accepting that Jesus actually died for me and that I was special enough and worthwhile enough for Jesus to do such a tragic thing for *me* was the hardest thing."

Georgie advises that the new Christian should never forget that they are precious to God.

"God made you special—he loves you and wants you."

She has two strong memories of her early days as a Christian: a sense of God's power and control over her life, and her marriage becoming closer and happier. But her husband Barry remembers periods when Georgie was ready to throw it all in.

"She often became very angry with God and didn't want to know him for a short while, but God doesn't let people go. Having faith in this encourages you in your lowest times."

What was the hardest part of being a new Christian?

"My first year as a Christian was amazing, but I did find

that some of the stories in the Bible seemed cruel and it was hard to accept that this was from a gentle and loving God. At first, all you want to do is read the Bible. But it was easy for my reading to become unstructured and confusing.

"It was also difficult to fit into church. It seemed like a closed club. However, some people made a real effort to show God's love to me."

And what were the highlights?

"Private prayer was great. God was never too busy and you could just talk and talk. And evangelism was, at first, very exciting. You want to tell the world—unfortunately, your knowledge is limited!"

Georgie's second year as a Christian was much tougher and less exciting. She often wondered whether she would be able to keep going. But, looking back upon her time, she can see that God was always at work in her life, bringing her to a deeper understanding of him and changing her to be more like his Son.

"My love for God has become stronger, but I tend to keep it to myself more. I tend more to live my life simply from day to day, and I really *want* God to take control. I know for certain now that, one way or another, God will do what God will do. I may as well listen to him and be prepared for anything to happen next!

"The best thing about becoming a Christian was realizing that God takes care of everything. You are not alone when you are with God."

GOD AND MONEY

The best things in life are free
But you can keep them for the birds and the bees
Just give me money.

The Beatles said it and most of us believe it. If there is one thing that might unite Australians, it's the belief that more money and more possessions equals a better life.

Developing a different attitude towards money is one of the most difficult changes that a new Christian has to make. It generally remains a problem all the way through your Christian life. It has been said that the last parts of a person's anatomy to get converted are the hip pocket nerve and the right foot (you know—the one you plant down on the accelerator).

Getting your attitude to money and possessions right early in your Christian life can save you a lot of stress and confusion later on. There are four major questions that we want to answer and they are certainly questions which the Scriptures address.

1. What is the place of money and possessions in the Christian life?

The fundamental teaching of the Bible in this area is that "the earth is the Lord's and everything in it" (Psalm 24). Nothing that we have is really ours because God created it and therefore it all belongs to him. Since he is ruler of all, we can only think of ourselves as managers or stewards of the world that God has given us. This really disturbs our view of the world, since our society operates by the principle of personal ownership: gathering possessions for ourselves and saying that things are 'mine, all mine'.

Even Christians are tempted to think of some things as ours and some as belonging to God. But we cannot 'buy God off' by giving 10% of our net income to religious causes and then consider the other 90% as ours to use however we wish. We are responsible for the way we manage *everything* we have. The Bible constantly reminds us that we are accountable to God for all of our actions, including the way we use our money and possessions. This is particularly important to Western Christians because we have been blessed with so many material goods.

2. How much should we give?

After we recognize that we only have money and possessions as gifts from God, we can work out *how* we should manage these gifts. The Scriptures make some very clear and somewhat surprising comments about earning, spending, giving and the connection between riches and happiness.

The practice of the faithful Israelite in the Old Testament was to give the first fruits of the harvest as a thank offering to God. Because God was so gracious in looking after the needs of his people, they were to respond generously. They were also obliged to tithe their crops each year (that is, give 10% to God), and this produce was used to support the priests who worked in the temple, as well as orphans and widows.

In the New Testament, this attitude of generosity is reaffirmed. But the practice of tithing is *not*. Christians are not under a law to tithe. Instead, we are to be generous all the time. Generosity should become our law, because we are thankful for everything God has done for us. Paul teaches this attitude in 2 Corinthians 9:6-8:

> Remember this: Whoever sows sparingly will also reap sparingly, and whoever sows generously will also reap generously. Each man should give what he has decided in his heart to give, not reluctantly or under compulsion, for God loves a cheerful giver. And God is able to make all grace abound to you, so that in all things at all times, having all that you need, you will abound in every good work.

Our generosity should extend to looking after the physical needs of others—believers and non-believers—and generously supporting the work of the gospel (evangelism and church work). We can look at the tithe as an indicator of where generosity starts, but we shouldn't feel that we are restricted to giving 10%.

3. Whom should we give to?

God gives us a fair amount of room on this question, but here is some accumulated wisdom which you might find useful. Firstly, take into account your understanding of the importance of people hearing about Jesus. We could give our money to any person in need or any organization involved in doing good works. But remember that, as Christians, the best deed that we can see done is someone being saved. This will influence our decisions about where to give. There's nothing wrong with supporting a dog's home, for example, but since only Christians will be supporting gospel organizations, we should be careful to give priority to this.

So how do we choose amongst the multitude of Christian groups, all doing gospel work of one kind or another?

- Your local church needs supporting. They are the people who teach, encourage, correct and train you. You benefit from this ministry, so it is only right that you help to finance it. Remember that your minister is not a public servant—no government payouts here. And there's no reason why his standard of living should be any different from yours.

- Overseas work is also important. God prepares some people to be involved in evangelism to other countries and cultures. Some people translate Bibles into foreign languages; others teach the Bible to the native Christians; others are evangelizing in places where the gospel has never been heard. Your local church probably supports certain missionaries, who may have come out of your congregation. These people need both money and prayer (not to mention letters).

- People often give to organizations or people that were influential in their conversion. If you got saved by reading a Bible that you ripped off from a hotel room (don't laugh—it happens!), then you might support the Gideons or the Bible Society. Organizations like that will probably send you a list of things they would like you to pray about.

Two final tips on giving: do it *regularly*, so that the organization that you are giving to can plan their budget more efficiently, and do it *without drawing attention to yourslf* or you may start to take pride in what you are doing. That is a sure-fire way to destroy pure generosity, which is what God really loves.

4. Will money and possessions make us content?

We are always just a couple of zeros short of the bank balance that we desire. If only we could get those few extra possessions, then we would be content. Or so we think. But we really have been sold a lie. It has to be a lie, because the people who *do* have the things that we hanker after *still* feel the same way that we do!

It is a constant temptation to believe that happiness will be found in the things we own and the power that money gives us. From our earliest years, our culture has impressed this idea upon us and keeps needling us through the all-pervasiveness of advertising. Part of our struggle to remain faithful to God is to resist this pressure. This really is a hard ask.

The Bible never states that it is wrong to be affluent or to enjoy this life. However, one of Jesus' strong themes is that it is foolish to seek happiness in material things (e.g. Luke 12:13-34; 16:1-15; 18:18-30). He tells us that the main priority for our lives needs to be the kingdom of God. If our values are the same as God's values, we will see that the things of the world are fleeting; they give us short-term pleasure and short-term contentment, but nothing that lasts. We will pursue the things that have eternal value and will satisfy—the truths and promises that we are taught in God's word. Paul gave this advice to his Christian friend, Timothy:

But godliness with contentment is great gain. For we brought nothing into the world, and we can take nothing out of it. But if we have food and clothing, we will be content with that. People who want to get rich fall into temptation and a trap and into many foolish and harmful desires that plunge men into ruin and destruction. For the love of money is a root of all kinds of evil. Some people, eager for money, have wandered from the faith and pierced themselves with many griefs.

1 Timothy 6:6-10

Put God and his kingdom first in all of your financial decisions and you may be surprised to find contentment.

CHAPTER 3

LIVING GOD'S WAY

DEAR DAVE

Greetings once again. Have you realised that it's your anniversary? By my reckoning it is exactly two months since something miraculous happened in your life! How does it feel? What—no cake and candles? My guess is that it's beginning to feel a tad familiar and a little bit ho-hum. Aren't humans marvelous—even the most incredible events can be taken for granted after a while.

But do not fear. It's normal. Many Christians go through a time of great elation after being saved and it feels like they will be on an emotional high forever. And yet a couple of months down the track, the feelings have gone and life rolls on as before.

And so we are left on the long, hard slog of the Christian life. I suspect you are beginning to find that life as a Christian is not all easy. In the great spiritual football game, sometimes you just have to put in the hard yards. To put it another way, being a Christian is sometimes difficult, Dave. We know what the right thing to do is, we want to do it, and yet it is a constant struggle. Why? It seems as if there is a conflict inside us when we become Christians. From your last letter, I gather that you are finding it particularly hard in your relationship with your family.

You are discovering what the apostle Paul wrote about in Galatians 5:25, which says, "Since we live by the Spirit, let us keep in step with the Spirit". When you became a Christian, God put his Spirit inside you. You have a new nature—you are a new creation. God's Holy Spirit lives in you and pushes you in an entirely new direction. The Spirit causes you to live in a way which pleases Christ.

Have you noticed that since you became a Christian you have actually wanted to live God's way? You can only want to do this because God has given you his Spirit.

But here is the catch. As a new person in Christ, you now have two sides to your nature. There is the new side, your spiritual nature. But there is also the side you always had—the sinful nature that is opposed to God. Once upon a time (i.e. two months ago), you were entirely controlled by that nature. Sin was boss in your life. However, you now experience a conflict between doing what the Spirit wants you to do and what your old, sinful, human nature wants you to do. All Christians experience this. Our struggle is to keep in step with the Spirit; to live the way God wants us to.

Dave, I don't mean to be rude but I do mean to be personal. When you had that argument with your father last weekend, would you say that you were acting as Jesus wanted you to act? I believe you when you say that you didn't start it, but that is not really the point. In Galatians 5, Paul explains what the Spirit wants us to be like—to be patient, joyful, peaceful, kind, loving, good, faithful, gentle and self-controlled. It is perhaps not a spectacular example of self-control or love to tell your father that he is a stupid jerk... I'm not disputing that he is. The point is, do you think Jesus would have reacted in the same way you did?

Please don't be angry at me for being blunt. I know exactly how you felt, and I have done exactly the same thing to people. I'm certainly not perfect. But God's Spirit wants us to treat people in a loving way—even difficult, painful people like your father. We all know unlovely people—if not at home, then at work or amongst people that we meet socially. It is the difficult people who test us most. It is no big deal to be loving to people who are lovely. The test is for us to love the unlovely. Don't ever forget that that is exactly what Jesus has done for you and me.

In Galatians 5, Paul tells us about the sinful nature at work in us. It produces sexual immorality, hatred, jealousy, rage, ambition and drunkenness, amongst other charming qualities. Don't fool yourself—these are the things that we struggle against all our Christian lives, even older Christians like me. (By the way, I prefer 'mature Christian' to 'old codger'. I am not *that* old!)

It's part of what some people call 'the now and the not yet'. We have a real relationship with God now: we are forgiven by him now; we have now received every spiritual blessing that he has to give. And yet we live in the real world where we still struggle against our sinful natures each day. A time is coming when we will no longer struggle—that is, when we will be in heaven and our sinful natures will be taken away. But while we are here, we struggle.

Remember, God has not left us alone. Jesus gave us his Holy Spirit so that we can fight against our human nature. In the next few weeks, I will say a little bit more about how to fight that war. Basically, it involves using some of the weapons that Christ has given us, such as prayer and the Bible. The Holy Spirit works on us as we recognize areas of our life that we need to change. The Spirit works through the Bible to tell me what I need to fix up in my life. The Spirit works in my life as I ask God to help me change.

Here's a gentle hint. Start asking God to change *you* so that when you see your father next time, it will be Jesus who shines through, not your sinful nature. Read Galatians 5 too, so that the Holy Spirit can start changing you. And while you're at it, pray for me. I know a few difficult people, too...

Love,

Michael

SCOTT

AGE: 21

"I had to give up habits that had made me popular with my non-Christian friends. I couldn't keep doing just anything to fit in with the crowd. I had to draw a line between obeying God and being one of the boys."

Scott had a long connection with religion before he genuinely gave his life over to Christ. Like many people, he knew that there was something in it all, but just couldn't be bothered putting in the effort to sort things out.

"I used to live a sort of 'Sunday Christian' lifestyle. In other words, I would go to the local fellowship group and church, but I would live my own life during the week. This went on for about five years."

So, what happened to change the situation?

"One day I was walking down to the shops with a close Christian mate of mine, when he told me how the life I was leading was rotten. Just then, I realized that not only was I destroying my life, but also the life of another friend of mine who was doing the same thing I was. That night I did some serious praying and gave my whole life to Jesus."

For Scott, becoming a Christian meant changing a few basic attitudes and behaviours. Whilst he was glad to be siding with God, Scott recognized that his new faith had its price.

"Now life is a lot more meaningful and I am much happier, but I've had a few difficulties. I had to give up habits that had made me popular with my non-Christian friends. I couldn't keep doing just anything to fit in with the crowd. I had to draw a line between obeying God and being one of the boys."

Did he feel that this was all too hard?

"Well, it was definitely difficult, especially with my workmates. As a young Christian, I wasn't very confident, but having the support and encouragement of Christian friends really pushed me along the right path and helped me grow.

"The thing that gave me the most trouble was my mouth. Trying to stop my mouth from producing foul language was much more of a challenge than I had expected. Oh, and giving up getting drunk."

When someone starts to believe the gospel, they often discover that reading the Bible for the first time is an eye-opening experience. What was it like for Scott?

"Reading it was hard at first, but I had friends who would do studies with me, which made things a lot easier. Now (two and a half years later), I have grown heaps in my Bible knowledge and have also found it a *bit* easier to read. My reading and praying times have become more frequent and meaningful."

Bible reading may have been hard, but Scott found that his prayers became "frequent and very thankful" and going to church "started to get better and wasn't as boring as I previously felt."

How would Scott summarize his journey as a follower of Christ?

"I have a better opinion of the people around me and a better outlook on life. I have had doubts at times, because I can't see who it is that I have given my life to. But those doubts fade away when I see all the great things Jesus has done for me and how his word fits into life. I realize how much Jesus really loves me, even after the life I led before becoming a Christian."

And what can he say to someone who is just starting out from where he was a few years ago?

"Hang in there, because our God is awesome. Becoming a Christian isn't going to be easy, especially when you will lose some non-Christian friends, but it is worth the struggle. The best thing is knowing that you are not alone and that you have a certain future with Jesus."

GOD AND SEX

1. The world's obsession

One glance across the magazine racks at your local newsagent will prove that our society is extremely interested in sex! Television revolves around it, movies glorify it, advertisers borrow its power. Sex is simply the world's obsession.

When we become Christians, we are commanded to live differently from the non-Christian world, and our sexual behaviour is one of the most obvious differences. Sex is still of great interest to us, but we are not to behave like non-Christians do. With sex, as with every other part of life, we are to obey God because we trust that he knows what is best for us. The Bible teaches some very clear truths about sex. Before we look at these, let's clear the air of some wrong ideas that many people believe.

2. Things people get wrong

Many people think that God is against sex.
They are wrong.
Many people think that sex is dirty in God's eyes.
Wrong.
Many people think that the original sin, the one that Adam and Eve did, was sex.

Wrong again.

Many people think that to really follow God they must never have sex.

Completely wrong.

Many people think that the only purpose of sex is for having children.

Wrong wrong wrong.

God is very much in favour of sex. In fact, he invented it. God designed us as men and women so that we could enjoy this special gift. When sex is used in the way God intended it, it is a powerful and pleasurable way of bonding a man and a woman. When this powerful gift is abused, it causes an enormous amount of harm.

3. A word about forgiveness

As a non-Christian, you may have done and thought and said a lot of things that you are now ashamed of. It is quite likely that the things you feel worst about have something to do with sex. Sexual sin is deeply harmful and it can leave you feeling very guilty, dirty and unlovable. But remember the message of the gospel—whatever sins you have committed, they are *all* forgiven because of Christ's work on the cross. No matter what sort of sexual sin you were involved in, God now considers you to be clean and pure. In God's eyes, you are acceptable and lovable. Your sin has been paid for and then left behind. God doesn't hold any grudges or secret anger towards you. Let it sink in— you are holy in God's sight!

If you do feel guilty and unclean, pray that God will forgive you your sins and help you to accept this forgiveness.

Then promise to make a fresh start with him, turning your back on the sin which used to engross you.

4. The purpose of sex

The Bible is full of talk about sex. It has practical advice, erotic poetry, commands to be sexually faithful, even a command to keep doing it. (OK, I'll tell you where it is—1 Corinthians 7:3-5). Right at the beginning of the Bible, God explains the place and purpose of sex. He creates the man, Adam, and places him in the garden of Eden. Everything God has created is called 'good', except for one thing:

> The LORD God said, "It is not good for the man to be alone. I will make a helper suitable for him."
>
> Genesis 2:18

Seeing that the man needed a partner, God created a woman, Eve, from Adam's side. He brought her to Adam, who was obviously very pleased with the new arrangement! At this point, we learn the place and purpose of sex:

> The man said, "This is now bone of my bones and flesh of my flesh; she shall be called 'woman', for she was taken out of man." For this reason a man will leave his father and mother and be united to his wife, and they will become one flesh. The man and his wife were both naked, and they felt no shame.
>
> Genesis 2:23-25

Sex is therefore part of the lifelong union of a man and a woman. Marriage is about leaving your home and setting up a new family. The purpose of sex is to bond this new family together so that they become 'one flesh'. Sex is being united into one body with your spouse, bonded together at the deepest possible level. You *leave* home and *cleave* to your spouse.

Sex is *also* for the creation of children. In Genesis 1:28, God tells Adam and Eve to multiply and fill the earth.

To summarize, the Bible teaches two purposes for sex. Firstly, it is the pleasurable bonding of lifelong partners. Secondly, it is for having a family. If you can't have children, sex is still a very important part of marriage, because it bonds you to your partner (and also because you enjoy it).

Because of the purpose of sex, it has to be enjoyed only within the lifelong union of husband and wife—in other words, any sex apart from sex between marriage partners is wrong in God's eyes. This isn't something that Christians have made up just to frustrate us all. It is what God clearly teaches in the Scriptures. In 1 Corinthians 6:9-10, the Apostle Paul warns us of God's attitude to sexual sin.

Everyone who continues to live in sin, sexual and otherwise, will be excluded from God's kingdom. Like the Corinthians, many of us have been involved in sexual sin. But, as verse 11 tells us, Jesus has washed away those sins and we can now turn our back on them. To our minds, which are so used to the sexual immorality of our society, God's views on sex can seem outdated and narrow-minded. But remember—God does not try to prevent us from having a great time; on the contrary, he wants to show us how to live the *genuinely* good life. And he does know what's best.

5. How to be sexually pure
Being sexually pure doesn't mean being celibate. It just means using sex in the right way, depending on your circumstances.

5.1 Marriage

If you are married, you must be completely committed to your partner. Any sexual activity with anyone else is strictly off limits. Jesus commands us to honour our partners, not only with our bodies but with our eyes as well (see Matthew 5:27-30). On the positive side, we are to give our bodies to our marriage partner in order to please them. We should not hold back from them sexually, because by getting married we have agreed to serve each other in this way (see 1 Corinthians 7:1-5).

5.2 Friendship

If we are not married, we must also be very caring in how we relate to each other. The Bible doesn't distinguish between friendship and 'going out'. It simply says that we are not to be sexually involved with anyone we are not married to. Look at the black-and-white way in which Paul instructed his friend Timothy:

> Treat younger men as brothers, older women as mothers, and younger women as sisters, with absolute purity.
>
> 1 Timothy 5:1,2

And in his letter to the Christians in Ephesus:

> But among you there must not be even a hint of sexual immorality, or of any kind of impurity, or of greed, because these are improper for God's holy people.
>
> Ephesians 5:3

The Bible makes it plain that the proper and good place for sex is marriage, and any sexual experience that we desire and seek outside of marriage is harmful to us (and the other person) and displeasing to God. In order to avoid these pitfalls, we should treat each other with the utmost purity.

6. But how far can we go?

Despite the clear teaching of the Scriptures, those of us who are unmarried still want to ask the question: "OK, what *can* we do?". It really is the wrong way to think. It is saying to God, "OK, we hear what you are saying but we want to get physical anyway and what we are doing isn't too hot, is it?".

God designed us with strong sexual desires, so he knows how we feel. And he does love us and wants us to enjoy this gift—that's why he instituted marriage. The answer to the question "What can we do?" is...get married first! But not all of us are in a position to get married, and we still go out with members of the opposite sex. Here are some suggestions for those of us in this situation.

1. Work out *why* you are going out with the person. Are you thinking of marrying them? Or are you enjoying a close friendship? Or are you just using them to make yourself feel loved and important? It sounds radical, but there are good reasons to think that, as adults, we shouldn't really 'go out' with someone if we can't imagine marrying them at some stage in the future. This doesn't mean that you have to propose on the first date (although it has been known to happen). It is just that relationships are serious business and we shouldn't treat them flippantly.

2. Realize that sexual activity outside marriage will confuse your relationship. Humans tend to bond to each other physically much faster than we bond mentally or emo-

tionally. Once you start becoming physically intimate, you are making it almost impossible to turn around and go back. If you do really love each other, you will want to keep each other pure, because this is how God loves us. And remind yourself that, if you don't marry this person, you are messing around with someone else's future husband or wife. You are causing someone else pain that could last a lifetime.

3. Make a distinction between *affection* and *arousal*. People say that the line you draw here will differ from couple to couple. But don't use that as an excuse to draw the finest line possible! Arousal is usually caused by touching the other person on a part that you haven't got.

7. That's impossible!

Some people become Christians and then find out that they have committed themselves to something where the guidelines for living seem impossible to follow. Christian living is so radically different to the culture that we live in. How will we be able to cope with the pressure that our workmates, our family and our partners will put on us to follow the way of the world instead of the way of God?

If you feel this sort of exasperation, take heart in the fact that Jesus underwent the same hardship and temptation that each of us faces as a Christian (see Hebrews 2:18). Turn to God in prayer for your strength, lean on your Christian friends for encouragement and advice and fill your mind with God's word instead of the world's word. How well we cope with our sexuality depends a lot on what we fill our heads with.

We must change our lives in the area of sex, and we have God's help to do so. It will take time for a new Christian to work through the implications of how God wants us to live sexually. Lots of painful changes may have to be made. But it will be worth it, because God wants us to fully enjoy sex as he designed it.

CHAPTER 4

LISTENING TO GOD

KICKING OFF

DEAR DAVE

Hello again and thanks for your letter last week. Sorry I've been slow in responding, but work at the office has bogged me down. But now I'm on top of things and keen to get on with more interesting matters!

Indeed, work seems to have been a tough issue for both of us. I'm sorry to hear of the difficulties that you have been facing. I was very proud of you when you said that you had told the guys at work that you were a Christian. That sort of thing is never easy, and we are always apprehensive about the response we are likely to get. And I think the response in your office is typical—some don't care one way or the other, some are quite interested and some are openly hostile. It's a shame that you have been nicknamed 'The Pope' by your workmates. Those little things can easily get under the skin and cause real anger and resentment. And yes, I do have some advice on what to do: cop it sweet. Turn the other cheek. Just let it go through to the wicket-keeper. You won't win any battles by getting angry. Grit your teeth, smile sweetly, pray earnestly and bear it. It is unpleasant, but there have been more painful forms of persecution in the history of Christianity. Lions would be much worse.

Take a look at 2 Timothy 3:16-17, which says absolutely nothing about work. It says: "All Scripture is God-breathed and is useful for teaching, rebuking, correcting and training in righteousness, so that the man of God may be thoroughly equipped for every good work". So why do I mention it?

All your friends at work have different opinions about God, probably ranging from blatant atheism to interest in the various religions of the world. Why should we be right and they be wrong? What makes us think that our opinions about God are worth anything more than theirs?

Well, here is the surprising answer. My opinions are worth as much as anyone else's, which is...not much!

But there is something amazing about the Bible. It doesn't claim to be a collection of smart people's opinions about God. It doesn't claim to be a series of brilliant observations about Jesus. It claims to be the word of God; the words that God spoke. Not my opinion about God, but God whispering his words into a person's ear (so to speak). The Bible lets us into God's own mind.

For instance, when Paul writes to slaves in Ephesians 6:7, "Serve wholeheartedly, as if you were serving the Lord, not men", he doesn't describe it as 'Paul's Handy Hints On Workplace Reform'. He is really saying, "God has told me to tell you this". You see the difference—I can give you all the advice I like, but you are at liberty to ignore it. But God speaking to you is an entirely different matter.

The Bible has authority because it comes from God. It is not a case of humans reaching up to God as they read, but God reaching down to us to tell us things that we would never know otherwise. And the Bible is sufficient—it has all we need to know to become the kind of people that God wants us to be. It is not lacking in any way. God hasn't left essential bits out. If the Bible doesn't mention something, then it's safe to assume that God is not particularly interested in it. And if it's in the

Bible, then we'd better sit up and take notice because these are the words of God.

So when someone says to you something like, "I like to think that God will accept everyone into heaven", what does this tell us about God? A big fat nothing. But it does tell us about this person, that they would rather make up an imaginary god than listen to what the true God is telling them loudly and clearly in the Bible. It's no surprise that these make-believe gods are always 'gods of convenience' who make no demands on our lives. It's what the Bible calls idolatry and God says he hates it. You can't make up things about God without him getting angry about it.

The Bible is a book to live by. It is not theoretical or impractical. It is vitally concerned with the way we live now. And don't ever get conned into thinking that it has become out of date. We might have drive-thru McDonalds now, but nothing has changed about human nature in the last two thousand years. Human beings have the same attitudes. It's just that, thanks to technology, we are now able to sin with greater efficiency! Once upon a time, if you wanted to kill someone you had to be in the same room with them to physically attack them. Now you can do it from across the other side of the world with the push of a button. Different methods, same sin. That's humanity for you.

The Bible is written to people like us. For instance, the Roman culture that Paul lived in was just as sex-obsessed as ours. When Paul writes about immorality he writes to people like us—same hormones, same desires.

Dave, if the Bible is God's word to us then we need to read it. I don't think I've said much to you about how to read the Bible, but if you are going to grow in your Christian life you need to start understanding for yourself how God wants you to live. That means Bible reading will need to be a priority in your schedule. I want to say more about the Christian tradition of 'quiet times' in the next letter, but let me suggest a few things now. Get hold of a Bible that you can understand easily. The Bible that your great-great-grandmother owned when she was on the First Fleet undoubtedly holds great sentimental value, but you won't understand much of it! The Bible hasn't changed, you understand, but the English language has. We don't talk like they did. The Authorized (King James) was published in 1611! The language is very poetic, but some words have completely changed their meaning since then. So get a Good News Bible or a New International Version Bible or a New Revised Standard Version of the Bible. (Just ask at a bookshop; they'll help you find one.)

Then start reading the Gospels. Perhaps 'The Gospel of Mark' would be best. It's the shortest of the four accounts of Jesus' life. Try to read a section each day, and think about what you've learned. Find a pattern of doing it—before breakfast or on the train or before bed-time. And try not to miss a day. I'll fill you in on more next time.

Love,

Michael

WARWICK

AGE: 30

"You've got to start taking what Jesus says seriously or else you can't really call yourself a Christian. If the Bible is telling me to stop worrying about tomorrow, stop putting money first and put God first, then I've got to do just that."

When Warwick finished university, he set off on a big overseas trip, not only to see the world but also to learn more about himself. It was a new stage in a spiritual journey that had been going on for some time.

"I'd felt an emptiness all through my teenage years. I'd filled it for a while with teenage relationships, but somehow they seemed to end in a confusing mixture of emotions. There was no inner peace and I was very aware of needing to find the answers.

"One of the most important things in my spiritual quest was when I studied yoga. I became interested in religion almost overnight—quite an inspiring experience. I studied other Eastern religions as well, but none of them gave me the answers. When I came back and settled down, I knew that I wasn't really satisfied. I wasn't really any different, although I might have thought that I was.

"Some guys I had gone to school with had become Christians. I knew in my heart that the answers were in the Bible. But for five years I sat on the fence, just toying with the idea of Christianity, trying to find the answers in myself, but really just going around in circles."

Warwick seemed to be searching for the truth. What was stopping him from genuinely enquiring into Christianity?

"Really, what was holding me back was the emphasis I'd put on my self-worth. I was threatened by Christianity and uncomfortable around Christians because I was forced to confront myself. I found the hardest part was letting go of myself as number one, letting go of my self-worth."

And when was the breakthrough?

"My wife and I wanted to get our son christened, so we went to the local church just as it was starting up. The minister there said the important thing is that you know what you're doing and that the christening is not a ritual. I thought I might have been a Christian at that stage, though I wasn't. He took an interest in us as individuals and started visiting our family on a regular basis, discussing the Bible and the person of Jesus.

"I was sitting on the fence but I knew there was a major decision that I had to make. In hindsight, I think I'd picked up some moral teaching from the Bible as a kid. I was quite a moral person really, but I knew something was missing. I know now what it was. It was Jesus. I saw an inner peace in Christians and I had an emptiness in me."

So, how did he know when he had actually become a Christian?

"I guess there is a moment when it happens, a moment when you let go or give in to God. You finally say, 'I've crossed the line, I'm yours. I'm willing to change. I'm willing to listen. I understand now in a small way what it's all about.' That moment of becoming a Christian was nothing spectacular, but the eight months that followed have not ceased to amaze me. It's been a gradual learning process. I have felt humbled, quite childlike."

A big part of the change that had come about in Warwick's

life was a new interest in reading the Bible to find out about God.

"I didn't really understand the Bible and its meaning, so I had to start reading it again. I had an awareness that I needed to learn what it's all about. I'd thought of the Bible as an historical document, but what I've learnt is that it's a document which is reliable. I see Bible reading as extremely valuable. I do see it as the word of God, showing me how to live my life.

"I've begun to understand things that I was blinded to in the past—basic answers to life. I've been looking for work relentlessly because I'm not very happy in my current situation. In the last few weeks, I've looked at the motivation for what I'm doing. Looking for good position, good salary, good career prospects and status are the wrong things to look for if you don't believe in what you're doing. You've got to start taking what Jesus says seriously or else you can't really call yourself a Christian. If the Bible is telling me to stop worrying about tomorrow, stop putting money first and put God first, then I've got to do just that. Now, all of a sudden, I'm looking at other areas."

What has it been like to pray?

"Prayer has been an awesome experience for me, being in relationship with God and being able to speak with him. I am aware of the presence of God on a personal level and also the presence of someone vast beyond description. Church has been very rewarding. It's very interesting to be part of a new church, a church that has no airs and graces—starting from scratch. I don't have very good memories of church as an institution. More than anything, I found it incredibly boring. I really like the youthful spirit in our church. It's got energy, and obvious signs of people who are positive about life."

And evangelism?

"I've become more accepting of evangelism. My early experiences of being evangelized by my friends were quite frightening. I went to this very large church—there was nothing humble about it. It was hard to handle some of the things they did, and I was frightened by the way they approached non-Christians. There was an incredible pressure on you to become a part of the church and you felt very different if you weren't. I didn't understand what motivated these people."

Warwick has undergone a complete change of direction and mindset, but he is still concerned about the future.

"There are moments when to be honest I just think, 'This seems so hard'. There are moments of temptation when I think about throwing it in. They can be really frightening, but they don't last long. It's so easy to fall back into the self-centred life. The trouble and concerns start coming back so that you think only of yourself. You can't become a Christian and expect it to all be wonderful. You've really got to work at becoming a better person. It's all about putting God first and everything else will follow. It's very easy to just go through life and fall into a comfortable mould and never really do the things that are right for you to do. But when God is in control, it's a source of great warmth and satisfaction—it fills the empty spaces in your heart.

"I feel the best part is still to come. The more I learn, the more my heart is filled. I believe that because of the Holy Spirit I will be a better person. I'll be better able to give love rather than take or lust after things. The emptiness has now been filled. I know this is right—I have no doubts about that. I have a relationship with God on a daily basis. I look forward to becoming wise as a Christian."

KICKING OFF

GOD AND WORK

1. Good or evil?

If you are blessed enough to have a job, you spend an enormous part of your life at work. It can be a time of great satisfaction or a cause of great conflict and aggravation. Almost everyone does some form of work, but people's attitudes toward their work are quite varied.

One person will see work as a drudgery which should be avoided at all costs. Another will call it a 'necessary evil' that is begrudgingly endured. A different point of view is that of the serious Young Achiever. The Y.A. is a workaholic who thinks that the work he or she does gives meaning to life. You can see these views of work in some of the stereotypes portrayed by the media—the incurably lazy public servant or the dole bludger or the workaholic executive, for example.

People who have these attitudes to work have all been fooled by the 'paradox of pleasure'. The paradox of pleasure is that the more you seek after pleasure, the harder it is to achieve. The more pleasure you want, the harder you have to work to get it. If your goal in life is leisure, then you will need to work like a slave. It's the myth of the 35-year-old retirement—"If I just work myself into the ground for 20 years, then I'll be able to relax and enjoy myself for the next 30." It's a lovely dream, but the reality of life without work is anything but pleasurable. Just ask anyone who is long-term unemployed.

On the other hand, the Y.A. is riding for a fall. If all your self-worth comes from your work, then corporate failure, sickness or retrenchment will be devastating. It's a fact of life— no-one is successful all the time.

To summarize: in various ways, we strive for satisfaction through our work, but end up frustrated. We need to work, but we also desire pleasure and, in this life, the two are in conflict.

God thinks that work is *good*. In Genesis 2:15, God gives Adam work to do. He charges Adam to look after the perfect garden in Eden, which has been made for his enjoyment. Work was, therefore, a part of life *before* sin tainted every human endeavour. Adam would have found work pleasurable and rewarding. It wasn't until *after* Adam and Eve had sinned that work become difficult and unsatisfying.

2. The working Christian

As Christians, we live in the last phase of history. We live *after* the Fall, and therefore our work is tainted by sin. But we also live *after* Christ has died to set us free from sin. How will our Christian faith affect our attitude towards work? In other words, what difference does Jesus' death make to the way we work?

When Paul wrote his letter to the new Christians in Colossae, he dealt with this issue. The Colossians were a group of people from all levels of society who had become Christians. They realized that they had to relate to each other in a new way. Before they were converted, some of them had been masters and some had been slaves. Paul explains that the differences between them have now been done away with. They are all one in Christ: "Here there is no Greek or Jew, circumcised or uncircumcised, barbarian, Scythian, slave or free, but Christ is all, and is in all" (Colossians 3:11).

All of their earthly differences mean nothing compared to their friendship in Jesus. This idea cut across the most basic division in the Colossian society—the division between the enslaved and the free. But notice that Paul doesn't argue either that slavery should be abolished or that it should be retained. Instead, Paul addresses their attitudes to whatever work they are doing. He tells slaves to do a good job for their masters and masters to treat their slaves well.

Because our relationship with God has changed, our attitude to other people at work should change too. That will include the people we work for, work alongside and those who work for us. We are told to treat our boss as if he or she was Jesus, who is our real boss:

> Whatever you do, work at it with all your heart, as working for the Lord, not for men, since you know that you will receive an inheritance from the Lord as a reward. It is the Lord Christ you are serving.
> Colossians 3:23, 24

It doesn't matter whether you work for the government or private enterprise, in a big or small firm, in management or on the shop floor. Whatever you do, do it in a way that serves Jesus.

By explaining things like this, Paul helps us to see that work is an act of *worship*. Worship is not just what we do at church during the singing—it is the way we live our whole lives. Everything that we do will reveal whether we think Jesus is worth following or not—that is, his 'worth-ship' (which is where the word 'worship' comes from). It's not just the 'religious' things that tell people what you think of God. It's every-thing that you do. The way you act every minute of the day expresses what you think of Jesus.

At work we often face opportunities to stab the boss in the back, or to rip-off the organisation a little, or to take a sickie from time to time. Since all these things are dishonest, we know that Jesus would not approve of us doing them. The question is, do we think that Jesus is worth following in these situations? Do I really care about Jesus? Is he really the boss of my life? Paul tells us to look beyond our earthly employer and to work as if Jesus is our boss—because he is!

3. Hard cases

Take a look at these two tricky work situations. They could easily be situations that you have already faced, or may be just about to meet.

3.1 Situation 1

There was a Christian who once worked in a hospital as a wardsman. One week, he told everyone that he was having a sickie the next day because he had to study for his Bible college exams. From his point of view, he was doing the right thing because it was the more 'religious' option. Guess what his workmates thought about his religion the next day as they coped short-handed with the same workload?

3.2 Situation 2

A Christian doctor was offered a partnership in the private practice where he worked. When he took a close look at the books, he discovered that the partners were involved in a very clever piece of medi-fraud. It was very lucrative and so well covered up that it would almost certainly never be discovered.

What would his boss Jesus want him to do?

Both of these issues deal with how we honour Jesus in our work. Both are about being honest and making ethical decisions. Decisions like these are continually on the agenda at work. The real test of our faith will be how we respond. Will we seek to always please Jesus first?

We looked at two examples for employees. The same problems (in fact more of them) face people who are in positions of power. As Paul told the Colossians, masters are to treat their slaves fairly, because they too have a Master in heaven. Translated into twentieth-century terms, employers who love Jesus will treat those who are under them with integrity and honesty. And this doesn't just apply to managing directors. If you have a team of people who report to you, or a secretary who works for you, or someone who buys your lunch, then treat those people with respect. Be fair, be patient, don't ask them to lie for you or use them as an excuse when you mess things up yourself.

The workplace can be a difficult environment to always serve Jesus, but it's also a great place to be a witness for him. Matthew 5:16 says "Let your light shine before all people, so they may see your good deeds and praise your Father in heaven."

And that's not a bad verse to use at work as our motto.

READING THE BIBLE

❖ Remember that you are reading the *word* **of God**. God is speaking to you as you read it. Before you start, pray that he will help you to understand his word.

❖ Make sure that you *own a translation that you can understand*, one written in clear modern English. (If your first language is not English, it is quite likely that you will be able to find a good translation in your natural tongue too). There are a number of good versions of the Bible and the New International Version (NIV), which many churches use, is one of the best.

❖ *Actually read it!* Set aside some time regularly, each day if possible, to get to know God better. Give up one television show or get up fifteen minutes earlier—however you do it, make sure you devote some time to learning from God's word.

❖ *Read it with your brain in gear.* Try to pick a time of the day when you are not exhausted (that is, *not* the very last thing at night). It does take concentration to read the Bible, so be sure to put some energy into it.

❖ *Read as much as you can manage.* People tend to only read a few verses at a time. This is a confusing and often unhelpful way to try to understand God's word. Reading through a whole book of the Bible in one sitting takes a bit of time, but it is a real eye-opener. You begin to understand the book as a whole, instead of in little bits. As a rule of thumb, aim to read a chapter a day.

❖ *Learn* **how** *to read the Bible.* The way you read a telephone directory is different from how you read a newspaper or a novel, because they are three different types of writing. Likewise, you need to know what sort of book the Bible is so that you will know how to read it. The Bible is one long story about how God has loved his people, but it is told in 66 different books! It traces God's involvement with humanity from creation right up to the end of the world. Obviously, there is a lifetime of reading between its two covers! Since the New Testament tells us about Jesus, new Christians usually find the New Testament the easiest place to start reading the Bible. The Old Testament is God's word too, but it can be a bit daunting if you don't understand the history behind it. (If you are Jewish, you may have a head start!) *The Gospel of Mark* is a short and simple record of Jesus' life, and is therefore a great first book to read. One of Paul's letters to the early Christians, such as *Philippians* or *Colossians*, is a good next step.

❖ The Bible teaches us about God and about how we should live to please God. After you have read a section, *ask yourself these questions*: "What do I learn about God and Jesus in this passage? How should I respond to what the passage is saying?"

❖ The Bible is also available on *cassette*—it's great to listen to in the car on the way to work or while you are washing the dishes. It's much better for you than the radio...and there are no ads.

CHAPTER 5

TALKING
TO GOD

DEAR DAVE

Spring-time always reminds me of exams. I can remember the days when I was studying—as the weather got warmer I'd be stuck inside reading a book, trying to learn large slabs of information. (One of my goals in life is to make sure that I never enrol in another course.)

So I can sympathize with you at this time of the year. I think part-time courses are the most difficult of all, and I hope you do well in your exams. I am praying for you, and indeed I want to talk to you about prayer. I was recently reading the book of Philippians and I was struck by Paul's words in chapter 4, verse 6: "Do not be anxious about anything, but in everything, by prayer and petition, with thanksgiving, present your requests to God". It seems particularly appropriate to your present situation.

Studying is a stressful activity because you have to cram in all that information before you get into the exam room. And who knows whether they will ask the things that you have learnt. When we're under pressure, we can be so busy trying to make things happen ourselves that we don't take time to talk to the One who is really in control. And that is the opposite of depending on God and the opposite of prayer.

Prayer is an unnatural activity. It doesn't come easily to human beings (it certainly doesn't come easily to me). As we spoke about once before, our sinful natures are always striving to be independent from God. But if we are going to keep in step with God's Spirit, then we will be people who pray, who admit our dependence on God.

Prayer is talking to God. He made us to speak to him. That's part of the wonder of prayer. Little children can talk to the Maker and Master of this universe and he hears them. In fact, I have found that my kids are great little pray-ers because they are familiar with depending on big people, like Mum and Dad. They understand prayer, which is all about depending on God.

Praying is an admission that God is in control and we are not. When I pray, I place God in his proper position. He is the boss who controls this world, and who makes things happen. I am just a creature, a being that he has made. I have to depend upon God. That is why I pray.

Paul says in Philippians that we should pray about everything. Nothing is too big or too little. God who is my Father is intimately interested in everything in my life. I needn't be anxious about anything, because God is in control. Being anxious about the events of this life is really stupid. All of my worrying really doesn't change anything. What I should be doing instead, as a Christian, is praying to God and asking him to sort things out.

Having said all that, I find that one of the big dangers of my prayer life is that it can become very selfish—the only thing I ever pray about is me and my concerns. God becomes the great vending machine in the sky, pumping out all the things that I want. Paul tells us to pray with thanksgiving, thanking God for all the great things he has given us. The greatest of all of these is Jesus' death for us.

In my last letter, I told you that God speaks to us in the

Bible. Prayer is how *we* speak to God. You can see how they naturally go together and Christians have developed the habit of 'quiet times' for that purpose. A quiet time is when you spend some time reading the Bible and then pray to God. It's nothing particularly magical or mystical, although it's incredible just the same—God speaking to you through the Bible, then you speaking to God in prayer.

Learning how to have a quiet time was one of the most significant developments in my early Christian life, because it meant that I could begin to grow in my knowledge and experience of God. It was probably the single biggest factor in 'growing up' as a Christian. So let me tell you what I do. This is not a law, but it works for me, and I suspect it might for you too.

The first thing I do is read a part of the Bible. I usually work my way through one book of the Bible day by day, so I can understand what that particular book is about. I like to read a chapter or so, slowly, so that I can think about what I'm reading. I ask myself questions: "What is God saying to me? Am I being taught something about Jesus? Am I being told how God wants me to live? Am I being warned about committing a particular sin?"

Then I pray. I use the 'A.C.T.S.' method that I was taught when I was first saved. There's nothing magical in it, but I think it helps me to approach God in the right way. A.C.T.S. stands for Adoration, Confession, Thanksgiving and Supplication (I think supplication is the only word they could think of that begins with 'S' and means 'asking').

First, I pray some prayers of *Adoration*—trying to think about who God is. I find it good to think of God's character— his power, his justice, his mercy. Sometimes I read one of the

Psalms from the Old Testament. Adoration prayers remind me that God is big and I am small. I need to depend on him.

This leads to *Confession*—confessing my sin. Despite the fact that we have been forgiven because of Christ's death, and been given God's Holy Spirit, we still sin. So we need to come before God and tell him that we have failed, and ask for his forgiveness, and seek his help so we won't do it again. That's what we do when we first become Christians, but it's also what we need to do every day.

Knowing that God forgives us leads to prayers of *Thanksgiving.* There is so much to thank God for, especially his generosity in sending Jesus to die for us. We can also thank him for answers to prayer.

And finally, I pray prayers of *Supplication*—asking God for different things. Doing this last means that you avoid praying 'gimme' prayers all the time. And these don't have to be self-centred either. Pray for yourself, but pray for others too. Pray that you will have more patience with your father; pray that he will be saved as well. I make it a point to pray for you every day. (Does that surprise you?) Pray that you will grow as a Christian, that you will get a chance to tell others about Jesus. There's really no shortage of things to pray about.

Here are a couple more hints. Try to have a quiet time every day. Some you'll miss—that's not the end of the world. But aim to do it every day. It really is such a privilege to speak to and be spoken to by God that you would be crazy to miss it. I have some cards on which I write the names of people I pray for. All my family are on one card, my work-mates on another and so on. I pray for the people on one card each day. I have some friends who have just moved to Paraguay as missionaries. They sent me a photo, so I keep it in my Bible and when I pray

I like to look at it—it helps to focus my prayers for them. My mind often wanders when I pray, so I often write my prayers out, just like writing a letter. I write 'Dear Father' at the top of the page, and then I start praying, just like I was writing a letter. It prevents my mind from wandering. With my mind, that is always a problem!

Dave, my prayer for you is that you will become a man of prayer. That you will want to bring everything in your life to God. That you will depend on him in all things. You might like to pray the same thing for me.

Love,

Michael

T   R   U   E   S   T   O   R   I   E   S

FRANCIS
AGE: 30

"It was only recently that I realized that praying tells you something about yourself, and that what you pray about reveals what you think is important."

Before she became a Christian 12 months ago, Francis's background was, as she describes it, "completely non-Christian; nothing". Her sister back in Holland had become a Christian some eight years previously, and it was regarded with some amusement in the family.

"All the same, I remember the last time that I went back to

visit my family in Holland, she got under my skin a little bit. I was still saying that it was all just 'so much rubbish', but I got to the point where I thought that maybe I should be a little more open-minded and have a look at it before I threw it away. I was also getting older and was starting to think about where my life was going (now that it was nearly half over). I got to thinking about what happened after; and if there *was* an after; and if there was, I wanted to be on the right side.

"These thoughts were going round in my mind, but I didn't actively pursue them. I went to do a course at tech and met a Christian man there who took me along to a Bible study, and that's how it all started. He was planted there to catch me!

"I listened to everything and tossed it all around in my mind for a while. I think what maybe persuaded me in the end was that the Christians I met lived different lives. I also got to thinking that in my family, out of all my brothers and sisters, only my Christian sister has been able to keep her marriage going. All the rest of us have split up. I began to wonder about this. What did she have that the rest of us didn't?"

Once she decided to become a Christian, Francis was faced with one particularly difficult decision: what to do about her partner? She had been living with this man for some time. The relationship was long-lasting, but he was not a Christian and didn't think much of Francis's newfound faith. She went to see her (new) pastor about it.

"He said to me, 'I won't help you with this problem unless you're prepared to do whatever is necessary to solve it God's way'. This was really the crunch, and I suppose that that was probably the hardest...five minutes, because it did only take me that long to decide that I wanted to do it God's way.

"Then he told me that, according to the Bible, I could stay

with my partner. He said that I hadn't had the wedding party but that I was effectively married to this guy and that I should stay with him."

As she looks back at the early months, Francis has strong memories of feeling inadequate and 'bad' as a Christian. Everyone seemed to know more than her; everyone seemed to be 'better' than her.

"When you become a Christian when you're 30 (like me) or 40 or 50, it adds to the feeling of being dumb. You'll end up in a situation where there's this 18-year-old Christian who knows so much more than you and runs rings around you. And the worst part is when you have to tell them that you don't understand what they're talking about. That can be fairly humiliating.

"Also, when you're with other Christians, you know your own past and you don't think that anyone else could have got up to the things that you did. But when you finally talk to some people about it—people who seem like really good people now—you find out that a lot of them got up to the same sorts of things before they were Christians. So when you open up a bit, you find that there are a lot of kindred souls out there.

"The funny thing was that although I felt like I wasn't much good when I was around my new Christian friends, it was my non-Christian friends who gave me the most trouble. At home my partner thought that I was becoming a bit of a goody-goody and not so much fun to be with anymore. And when people came round to dinner and talked about how they cheated on their tax return or went shopping in the median strip for plants, well…what do you say? You smile sweetly and say nothing, even though you disagree with their morality (or lack of it).

"Most of my friends were pretty surprised. I was the last person that they thought would do something 'silly' like that."

Despite feeling a little inadequate, Francis really enjoyed going to church. And she also enjoyed the security of knowing that she was known by God.

"For me, the best part about being a Christian is knowing that it doesn't matter any more what's going to happen to me, because I'm just not going to be alone. It used to be a big problem—being alone—but not any more. There are lots of good bits, but that's the best bit."

How does she find things like prayer?

"When I pray on my own, half of it's in Dutch and half in English, depending on which topic we're discussing at the time. I do find it hard sometimes because my mind wanders—all of a sudden you find that you're thinking about something completely different. And then you pull yourself back and start again. And also, it was only recently that I realized that praying tells you something about yourself, and that what you pray about reveals what you think is important. I've been analyzing that I need to pray more about some of the really important things, like people coming to Christ and so on."

And is there anything that she would really like to say to a new Christian?

"I recently discovered that when I finally end up telling other people how I feel, everyone else feels the same—even if they've been a Christian for 25 years. So I'd ask this question in my Bible study group and feel like it was a really stupid question, and then afterwards I find that two or three other people were also wanting to ask that question but weren't game to!

"It's also true that churches can be fairly cliquey, which is understandable because often they've all known each other for years. It isn't always easy to 'get in'. But if you go along to some small groups, you can meet some other people, and their friends and their friends, and so on. You need to do that."

TALKING TO GOD

❖ *Remember what prayer is—talking to God.* It isn't a ritual or a law that we have to obey. It is the way we relate to God. It is proof that we rely upon him. God is our loving father who is always delighted to hear our prayers. You can tell him whatever is on your mind.

❖ *Try to pray each day, at the same time that you read your Bible.* When you read a Bible passage, ask yourself: "What are 3 things that I can pray from this?". Pray at a time when you can concentrate best.

❖ Sometimes people find that when they come to pray, they can't think of what to pray. *Write out a list of people, organizations and events that you are involved with and pray about some of these each day.* You don't have to pray for them all each day—you can slowly work your way through the list. The advantage of being organized like this is that it directs your prayers.

Pray for your church, your unconverted friends, people in gospel ministry, those in authority over us, for justice and righteousness in this country. Pray for anything and everything, no matter how big or small.

❖ Should you pray out aloud or to yourself? It doesn't matter—God hears both. If you are by yourself, *praying out loud can be a help* because it stops your mind from wandering.

❖ If you have trouble concentrating, *try writing out your prayers.* Buy a notebook, write the date and 'Dear Father' at the top and then note down all that you want to say, just as if you were writing a letter.

❖ When praising God in your prayers, you might like to *use the words of a hymn or chorus or psalm.*

❖ *Try using the A.C.T.S. method*, which was outlined in the letter.

CHAPTER 6

MEETING WITH GOD'S FAMILY

KICKING OFF

DEAR DAVE

You must be ecstatic about finishing your exams. It really is a very good feeling, isn't it?

But now that you are finished, I want to raise a subject with you that has been on my mind for a while. You've mentioned a few times that you have been to church, but I get the impression that you really visited a few different places rather than actually joined a church. Now there's nothing wrong with visiting churches, but the Bible does have some important things to say about why we belong to a church and what we are supposed to do there. So now is as good a time as any to look at them.

Hebrews 10:24-25 says:

> And let us consider how we may spur one another on to love and good deeds. Let us not give up meeting together, as some are in the habit of doing, but let us encourage one another—and all the more as you see the Day approaching.

It is one of the clearest New Testament teachings on why we go to church, so it's worth spending some time looking at it.

The writer is saying that the reason we go to church is to encourage one another; in other words, to help one another live the Christian life. You know as well as I do by now that being a Christian is not easy and you need all the help you can get. That is why one of God's gifts to us is *other Christians* that we can meet with to help us keep growing.

Going to church is essential if you want to continue as a Christian. You hear people all the time saying, "I don't have to go to church to be a Christian". And, in one sense, that's true. Going to church doesn't make you a Christian anymore than going to McDonalds makes you a hamburger.

But think about it from a different point of view. What would you say if I told you I was a Rugby League fan, but that I never went to a game, never watched it on TV, never listened to it on the radio or read about it in the papers or spoke to any other League fans. I think you would have to seriously doubt my level of interest.

What do you think of people who say, "I'm a Christian, but I don't need to go to Church"? They can't be fair dinkum! I would've thought that if Jesus was the most important person in your life then you would be busting to find out how to follow him better.

I can't see how you can be a Christian and turn up your nose at the opportunity to meet with other Christians. It doesn't make sense to me. Certainly, the Bible never talks about people being Christians by themselves. The writer of Hebrews wants us to keep on meeting, so that we can spur one another on. I always think of those old cowboy movies, the guys with the spurs on their boots. And sometimes, Dave, I've needed a boot when I was straying from what God wanted me to do. Because I was meeting with other Christians and they cared about me enough to look after me, they actually gave it to me.

In the New Testament, 'church' is not a building; church is a gathering of people who encourage one another to serve the Lord Jesus. Acts 2:42-47 gives us a clear picture of what the first Christian church did. They met together often, they listened to Bible teaching, prayed for one another and looked after one another, even financially. It says they often ate together too (funny how church and food always seem to go together).

These days there are lots of different brands of church on the market, such as Anglican, Presbyterian, Baptist, etc. These are groups of individual churches organized together into 'denominations'. What churches believe can vary a lot even within the same denomination. Unfortunately, just because there's a sign out the front that says 'Church' doesn't mean that these people teach or believe the truth. Does this sound confusing? It is.

Mate, you've got to find a good church and join it. I don't know the churches in Cedargrove, but I can suggest a few important things to look for as you check them out.

I don't actually care so much about the brand you choose, whether it's Anglican, Baptist, Presbyterian or whatever. Every denomination has good and bad churches. But you need to find a church where the Bible is well taught. By that I mean, do they open the Bible and teach from it in their church meetings? Are you learning about Jesus when you go there, and being encouraged to serve him? If the leaders of the church don't take the Bible seriously and teach from it, don't join that church. People need to be friendly to one another but that's not enough. You can find friendly people at your local bowling club, but it's important that Christian fellowship be based on God's truth in the Bible. One way you can tell if they take the Bible seriously is by their attitude to you when you visit and their attitude to each other.

The church that I go to also has smaller groups that meet during the week to study the Bible and pray. Most good churches have them, and they're great. In our group we get together each Wednesday night. One person leads a study on a part of the Bible and we discuss what we have learned and how it applies to our lives. Then we tell each other the things we need prayer about, and we pray for each other. We try to pray about those things during the week too.

I think about them as big church and little church, and each is important. Big church is good for meeting lots of other Christians, for hearing good preaching, for praying about the broader concerns of church life. But little church is good for meeting together at a personal level and sharing things with people who know you. In the time that I've been in this group, we have got to know each other well, and some people have really helped me to keep on the right track in my Christian life.

The passage from Hebrews talks about us continuing to meet "as the Day approaches". He is talking about the Day of the Lord, the day when Jesus returns to judge the world. We don't know when that will be but I guarantee it will be one year closer than last year. It seems a funny thing to mention, doesn't it? Well, he does it for a reason. He is concerned that his friends don't just kick off as Christians, but that they keep on going right through to the end, until the Lord's return or until they die, whichever comes first. And one way to keep going through the difficult times is to receive encouragement from the people you meet with at church.

Even when you find the right church, I know sometimes you'll find it hard work. If you feel this way, you're not Robinson Crusoe. A mate of mine once said, "You'll never find a perfect church and if you do, don't join it; you'll only muck it up". As a Christian, you are part of God's family and you can't choose your relatives. You need to be committed to the people in your church, even if sometimes you don't feel like it.

The writer of Hebrews says, "*Consider* how we can spur

one another on". We've got to use a bit of brain power to decide how best to do it. Here are some suggestions. Find a good church and become a regular member. Join a Bible study group. Get to know other Christian people and begin to think about how you can encourage them to serve Jesus. Get started and let me know how you get on.

Love,

Michael

T   R   U   E   S   T   O   R   I   E   S

DOMINIC

AGE: 26

"One of the best parts of being a Christian is the relationships. I'm just starting to understand that promise of Jesus when he says, 'If you give up everything and follow me, you'll get a hundredfold increase in homes, mothers, fathers, brothers, sisters'."

If you have seen those fish stickers that some Christians have on the back of their cars, you might have thought they were pretty daggy. And you might have been right, but a fish sticker helped Dominic become a Christian.

It all started in about 1983 when Dominic left the big city for a job in country radio. When he returned, 18 months later, he went back to the Catholic Church where he'd been a keen member since his childhood (he was even an altar boy).

"They didn't realise that I'd been away for 18 months. The message was fairly clear—I didn't really matter to these people. My ego couldn't cope, so I left."

How did he become a Christian? Like many people, for Dominic it was a combination of things—including the fish sticker.

"A Christian girl, whom I was chasing at the time, bought me a book called *How to be a Christian Without being Religious*. I can't say I've ever read it, but it at least gave me the idea that such a thing was possible. She also sold me her car, which had a fish sticker on the back window. This left me in a dilemma. I'd rejected Catholicism, but should I take the fish sticker off the car? To go out one Saturday morning and razor-blade off the fish sticker was really to say, 'Get lost, God. I'm just not interested'. But to leave it on was a constant niggling reminder that I was being a hypocrite.

"One day, a Christian workmate called Russell was talking with me in the carpark. I showed him my new Celica (which I was very proud of) and he said, 'What's the go with the fish sticker?' I told him that I couldn't decide whether or not to take it off.

"He said, 'Why don't you come along to our church—it might help you make up your mind'."

Dominic didn't make it to the church for three weeks, but when he did turn up Russell was out the front of the church on the footpath waiting for him, 10 minutes after the meeting had started.

"I was tremendously impressed, because I knew that for the last three weeks he had been out there for 10 minutes after the meeting started, waiting for me. He was very welcoming and invited me back to his place afterwards. Here was a place where Christianity looked sensible and credible."

It was some months later at a convention that Dominic knew that he was a Christian. He's unsure exactly when or where the decision was made, but somehow it was. The speaker at the convention had some strong things to say: "The Christian life is a long-distance race, and you can't run a marathon with rocks in your pockets. So if you're going to be a Christian, take the rocks out of your pockets and take off the overcoat too. If it's getting in the way of you serving Jesus, get rid of it."

Dominic remembers what happened next quite clearly.

"I drove straight from the convention to my non-Christian girlfriend's place. She said, 'So what you're saying is that either I become a Christian or we stop going out together'. I said, 'No it's worse than that. You've got to become a Christian full-stop, because it's true.'

"So we stopped going out together. She thought about it and talked about it and ended up becoming a Christian some months later. I'd like to say that there was a happy ending to the story, but we finally broke up three years later and she's now married to someone else."

What was the hardest thing about deciding to become a Christian?

"The big problem was admitting that it was not *me*; that it was God's work; that I had nothing to contribute; that it was by God's grace not my works. The other thing that was very hard was dealing with my girlfriend. It was a tremendous struggle to change our behaviour. I'd be very firm now about people breaking up with their non-Christian girlfriends/boyfriends.

"I went through tremendous agony trying to decide: non-Christian girlfriend or God? But I knew that if I didn't go with God it would constantly eat away at me, because I knew it was true, whereas I didn't know if my relationship with my girl-friend would be long-term.

"Another struggle was my lack of regularity in church. This girlfriend lived in another city and I was also doing shift work; so between those two things, I missed a lot of Sundays and Bible study groups. I just didn't get to know people. When my circumstances changed and I started to meet regularly with other Christians, that's when I really started to make some progress and grow."

And what were the best things?

"One of the best parts of being a Christian is the relationships. I'm just starting to understand that promise of Jesus when he says, 'If you give up everything and follow me, you'll get a hundredfold increase in homes, mothers, fathers, brothers, sisters'. I can now see people who treat me like a son or a brother. My relationships are just so much richer and wider than the ones my non-Christian friends have—and that's not counting my relationship with God!

"Looking back then, I remember the relief of knowing that I was 'comfortable' with God. With Catholicism, I always thought that something else was required, that there was something lacking."

Like many new Christians, Dominic found going to church just a little strange at first.

"It was a huge culture shock going to a gospel-centred church. There were no candles, none of the religious trappings, and yet people at this place were taking God more seriously. What's more, they were only there because they *wanted* to be there—this made a big impression on me. People at this place were keen and committed; they didn't leave straight after com-munion like many did in my old church.

"It was still hard to fit in at times. I remember standing at church one night after the meeting was over, and everyone seemed to be talking to someone, but no-one was talking to me. I felt, 'Do I fit in here?'. I also remember times when I didn't feel like going to church. I don't think I ever felt that I was not a Christian, or that I wanted to throw it all in. I was just slack from time to time."

What would be Dominic's advice to a new Christian?

"Check out that your church is teaching you the truth, and then make sure you go...regularly! The other thing is: find a friend who can encourage you and answer your questions, who'll be around for a while and help you out."

P R A C T I C A L   T I P S

GOING TO CHURCH

❖ *Remember the good reasons for going*—to be encouraged, to keep going in the Christian life and to encourage others to do the same.

❖ *Forget the bad reasons for going*—you don't go to church in order to get closer to God, to pay your dues to him or to keep up your respectable reputation with your neighbours!

❖ *Choose one church and go to it.* Which church? One where the Bible is well taught and where the leaders and the congregation love Jesus. You can see this most clearly by whether they take the Bible seriously and apply it in their daily lives. You may need to visit a few churches before you find one that fits the bill.

❖ *Go to church even when you don't feel like it.* Church is not an optional extra, like beetroot on your hamburger. It is essential. It's hard to imagine someone who loves Jesus and doesn't want to meet with Jesus' people. It's almost impossible to survive on your own as a Christian. You need the encouragement of others and they need you. Make it a priority to be there every week.

❖ *Go with the right attitude.* You will hear God's word explained, you will praise him and encourage others in song, you will pray with your brothers and sisters to your Father, you will support your church financially because gospel work is so important. What could be more important than all that? So go with a positive attitude.

❖ *Remember your purpose while you are at church.* You are not just there to have your needs met, but also to meet the needs of others. Be encouraging to other people, be friendly to visitors, look out for lonely people, talk about Christian things over coffee, don't gossip about people.

CHAPTER 7

MEETING THE WORLD

KICKING OFF

DEAR DAVE

I suppose this letter will be waiting for you when you get back from holidays. I hope you had a great time and didn't get too sunburnt.

I got the letter you wrote to me just before you left. I'm pleased to hear that you've found a good church. One Sunday I'll try to get out there and go with you. It's also great to hear that there have been a few hot discussions about Jesus at work. Matthew sounds like a real hard case, but don't be disheartened. Sometimes the people who get a bit aggro are the ones who God is really working on. I know you haven't been able to answer all his questions but telling someone the gospel is a bit like being thrown in a pool—you might swallow a bit of water, but you'll learn to swim pretty quickly.

After I got your letter, I started thinking—I've been a Christian for about 12 years now and I don't have many non-Christian friends. I'm actually in danger of bricking myself into a comfortable Christian ghetto. I've decided that I'm going to make a big effort to get to know more people at work, visit a few of my neighbours and maybe even invite them over for a meal so that I can talk to them about Jesus.

All of this made me realize it was about time I talked to you about evangelism. In the New Testament, evangelism means 'gospelling'—telling people the gospel. It means telling people about Jesus and how they can be saved. It's what I did with you about eight months ago.

It's not hard to work out why evangelism is very important. To put it bluntly, if people don't believe in Jesus they are on their way to hell. As the book of Acts tells us, "there is no other name given under heaven by which we must be saved" (that's in Acts 4:12).

We don't evangelize because of duty or guilt, but like everything else in the Christian life, the motivation is love. Because Jesus first loved us, we love other people. And if we love them we will want them to hear about Jesus.

I can't show you a Bible verse to prove it (that may surprise you), but in my experience evangelism is almost always 'truth shared in relationship'—that is, someone you know and trust telling you about Jesus. Getting to know people in this way can be hard work.

The Apostle Paul had a great heart for evangelism. He was prepared to put himself out for other people so they could hear the message of Jesus and be saved. Here are a couple of verses from his first letter to the Corinthians (10:33-11:1):

> I try to please everybody in every way. For I am not seeking my own good but the good of many, so that they may be saved. Follow my example, as I follow the example of Christ.

Paul gave up rights and privileges so that he could get on with all kinds of people—not to be a crawler or social climber, but so that he could tell them about Jesus. It cost him plenty—his health, his career, his freedom and eventually his life. It wasn't any easier for him than for us. And he calls on Christians to follow his example of costly service to others. He followed the example of Jesus, who is the greatest example of self-sacrificing love.

So what does this mean for us? Evangelism means putting yourself out for people who haven't heard the gospel. It means building a relationship with people where your goal is to tell them about Jesus. The relationship is like a bridge—it's no good building it if you don't get around to crossing it. Making friends with people is good, but it's not evangelism. Evangelism requires communication—you've got to actually tell them the message. They won't pick it up by osmosis.

Let's talk about our mate Matthew. I know he's a pain and a know-all, but that is not the point. You have to love him and, yes, I know that is very hard. But Matthew needs to hear about Jesus just like you did, and I might point out that in the first conversation you and I had about the gospel, your enthusiasm wasn't exactly overwhelming. And by the way, the bloke who led me to the Lord had to put in some hard work too. Loving Matthew means praying for him, looking for opportunities to talk about Jesus, even doing things with him. Does he play squash? Then play a game with him. If he doesn't, he must want to eat sometime.

But make sure you remember this. He is not just a project or a scalp. He's a person, who needs friendship and love and Jesus. He doesn't deserve those things but neither did we. Evangelism and love go hand in hand.

What about your Dad? I think relatives are the hardest ones to share with, because they know you so well. Your Dad knows your weaknesses and faults, and it's hard to tell someone about the meaning of life when he is thirty years your senior. But hang in there, and keep praying.

The quality of your Christian life either gives you great credibility or none at all. No-one will be interested in your message if you don't convey some of the joy of the Christian life. Or if you lack integrity. Why would anyone listen to the message of a hypocrite? On the other hand, living a good life is not enough either. I once worked with a woman who was Christian and godly and enormously well-liked. But because she never told people that it was because of Jesus that she lived the way she did, the glory went to her and not the Lord. What we say and how we live have to fit together.

One last thing, Dave. There are some ways to get better at evangelism. I read a book called *Know and Tell the Gospel* by John Chapman. It was very good and easy to read. I also did a course they ran at our church to learn a gospel outline. It was called *2 Ways To Live*. It gave me an outline of what to say when I had a chance to speak to someone about Jesus. You could check out either or both of these.

See you soon, and I'll be praying about Matthew.

Love,

Michael

T R U E   S T O R I E S

MAL

AGE: 24

"I always believed in God and knew Christianity was the right thing. But if someone said 'Put up your hand all the Christians', it wouldn't have gone up."

Friendship was the main factor in Mal's conversion. He really wanted friendship with God, but he knew there was a cost involved. In the end, he decided that he didn't want to be alone. So he accepted a relationship with the One who is always there for us.

Mal has been a Christian for six years, although he grew up in a Christian family.

"As I look back on it now, my mother was very influential. I had a very happy childhood, I enjoyed life so much and I wanted it to last forever. But I had dreams about dying, everything turning black and then nothing. I remember going crying to Mum, saying 'I don't want to die'. She said, 'You don't have to'. She taught me this Bible verse: Isaiah 41:10, 'Do not be afraid, for I, the Lord your God, am with you.' It stuck with me all through school."

The event that tipped the balance toward God occurred at the end of 1985—Mal's first year after school. It was the departure of his girlfriend.

"She went overseas, and I was alone. I realised the only way I could never be alone was to put my trust in the One who would never leave me. Now I love spending time by myself. It's real quality time with God, never alone."

But the decision to become a follower of Jesus wasn't easy. The hardest part was acknowledging Jesus' control over his life.

"I have the kind of personality where I like to feel in control of what's happening to me. When I was 17 or 18, it was a very exciting time in my life. I was playing NSW under-19 cricket with some people who are now playing for Australia. I was virtually sponsored, a semi-professional, receiving match payments if I did well, getting advice on training. People were pushing me, telling me I was very talented. I loved cricket, but it got to the stage where I was no longer in control. It forced me to ask some questions about what I was doing and where God fitted into it all. It made me think about whether God was in control of my life. I wanted to go on and play cricket for NSW and Australia, but I had to decide whether I was going to let God or my ambitions have first place."

He decided to make God top priority, but Mal found it quite difficult to face the possibility of rejection for his choice.

"I've always had trouble standing apart from the crowd. My personality makes me really look for social acceptance. I always believed in God and knew Christianity was the right thing and I always said I was a Christian when I was at school. But if someone said 'Put up your hand all the Christians', it wouldn't have gone up. Christians were dags in my view. I really wanted everyone to still accept me. I didn't find Bible reading or church or praying hard—I'd really grown up with it. The real stuggle was standing up for my faith, being able to say, 'Yes, I'm a Christian' and just trust God that it would be all right.

"It was hard, too, when all my mates were out drinking, having sex and having a good time. At the time my hormones were bouncing around. It's the closest I've come to packing it all in. I asked myself a lot of questions—What if I miss out on all this fun? Is being a Christian really worthwhile? I toyed with the idea of having my fun now and then coming back to Christianity when I was older. I thought, 'Even if I do have sex, God will forgive me.' I thank God that I've avoided that—I get more fun out of having a proper relationship with my girlfriend."

In his first year as a Christian, one event stood out for Mal.

"It was a youth group weekend away at Nowra. We had some great talks and I really enjoyed the friendship of the people there. We had a song session with a guitar, and I shared what I'd learnt from the weekend. I was saying all this stuff and I remember asking myself, 'Is this really me saying all this?'. It was a real buzz. I'd had some pretty good times, but this was great."

After a religious upbringing, what was it like for Mal to do all of those Christian activities as a true believer?

"Church was easy. I didn't feel threatened. I knew all the right things to do, all the tricks of the trade—even how to make people think you were listening to the sermon. (When I was really young, I took a transistor with an earplug during the sermon.) Bible reading wasn't hard. I'd grown up with it really. The only problem was that I'm pretty lazy and I don't read a whole lot of books. It was good when I actually got down to doing it. Prayer wasn't difficult either—I love to talk!

"But evangelism really threatened me because of my need for social acceptance—speaking to people who I knew were going to disagree with me wasn't my cup of tea. I'd do anything to avoid conflict. In fact, I still find it hard as a more mature Christian. I know it's really important and you do get better at it as you grow more confident in your relationship with God. I've found it really helpful to study the Bible—the more you know what it says, the easier it gets.

"Work can be difficult, too. I love a joke but I find myself laughing at things and then I think, 'I shouldn't be laughing at this and it's not funny anyway.' It's the social acceptance thing. In the same way, I like to tell a good story but sometimes it's too easy to exaggerate to the point where it becomes a lie. In the area that I work, being honest is hard, but I've told my boss it's the only thing I can do. Setting an example with your workmates is the hardest thing. You need to have their respect so that they will discuss Christian things with you. At work, I'm known as 'The Christian'. If I slip up, they're on to me. It puts a lot of pressure on me. I guess from that point of view, it's good too."

What should a new Christian expect to experience?

"When I first became a Christian, I thought it was great because I received so much. As I get more mature in the faith, I enjoy giving as well as receiving. I get a lot of pleasure from being involved in ministries at church, knowing that I'm doing it for Jesus, working for someone who sacrificed everything for me. My advice to a new Christian is firstly to enjoy it—coming to faith in Jesus is incredibly exciting, the biggest decision of life. For me, it's been a source of true contentment. I've got a girlfriend, I have some really good friends, but they can't 100% rely on me or me on them. But with God you can. And keep your eyes on the cross. Try to understand the implications of Jesus' death for us, because getting to know Jesus is what really changes our lives."

P R A C T I C A L   T I P S

TELLING OTHERS ABOUT JESUS

❖ *Know why you do it.* If the love of God has changed your life, don't you think it would be a good thing if other people knew about it too? And Jesus deserves to be known as Lord throughout the whole earth. These are our two great motivations.

❖ Remember it works. How do you think you became a Christian? *It's not you doing the work, but God who works through you.* This means that God can use your bumbling, nervous efforts to explain to a friend your faith in Jesus. We should never feel discouraged in speaking of our faith, because our powerful God is working through us.

❖ When you are explaining your faith, *talk about Jesus.* Topics such as going to church, praying to Mary or being a moral person are not the main issue. The main issue is whether Jesus Christ is Lord of your life. People need to hear about Jesus first and foremost—the other things can be discussed later.

❖ *Ask the minister at your church to teach you a simple way of explaining the Gospel.* Courses such as '2 Ways to Live' or 'Christianity Explained' are very handy. If your minister can't help you to do this type of training, or put you on to someone who can, perhaps you are in the wrong church!

❖ *Don't abandon all your non-Christian friends.* They've got to hear the good news from someone and it probably should be you. It's all too easy to throw yourself into your new Christian life and forget where you once were. Remember that you were like them not so long ago.

❖ *Have the right attitude.* Don't be a smarty-pants, don't be arrogant, don't be self-righteous. You have been saved by God's grace, not by anything you have done— so don't boast. In telling others about Jesus, love them in the same way that Jesus loves you.

❖ *Don't underestimate people's interest in spiritual matters.* Christians are often more reluctant to talk than their friends are to listen! People are often aware that there is something missing in their lives and may be just waiting to hear about what has happened in yours.

STEPPING OUT

Congratulations! You have made it to the end of the book. (Unless you are one of those people who read the last chapter first.) We trust that this book has been handy for you in kicking off your Christian life.

By now, we hope that you have begun to pray regularly, read your Bible often, attend a good church and meet with other Christians. We expect, too, that you are probably experiencing some discomfort, as God's Holy Spirit challenges you about your life and begins to change you. You are probably dealing with a long list of new issues—how to relate to your family and friends, how to behave in the workplace, what to do with your money. Don't give up—being Christian is a life-long challenge.

We wrote this book in order to help people like yourself get started as Christians because we both have a passionate belief in Jesus Christ. He has changed our lives incredibly and we hope he will do the same for you. If you want to drop us a line c/- St Matthias Press, to let us know how you are getting on and what you thought of the book, we'd be glad to hear from you—remember, you're part of the family now.

You've kicked off. Now it's time to step out. Your journey towards the goal has only just begun. Let's give God the final word, from the book of Jude, verse 24:

To him who is able to keep you from falling and to present you before his glorious presence without fault and with great joy—to the only God our Saviour be glory, majesty, power and authority, through Jesus Christ our Lord, before all ages, now and forever more! Amen.

Ed and Al
October, 1992

MORE RESOURCES FOR NEW CHRISTIANS FROM ST MATTHIAS PRESS

Just for Starters (now revised)

These seven basic studies are widely known as *the* material to use with new and young Christians. They were first developed as follow-up material for the Billy Graham Crusade of 1979 and have just been revised, with an improvement in layout/presentation and some fine-tuning of the content. They cover the same seven topics as *Kicking Off*, but in a Bible study format.

The Complete Christian (Colossians)

by Phillip Jensen and Tony Payne

What is the normal Christian life? What should Christians expect to experience? What does it mean to be fully and genuinely a Christian?

The Apostle Paul's short letter to the Colossians offers simple but marvellous answers to these questions. For new Christians who want to be sure that they're on the right track, or for longer-serving Christians who are bedazzled by the range of alternatives on offer, *The Complete Christian* sheds bright light from God's Word.

The Complete Christian contains six Bible studies suitable for group or individual use.

The Path to Godliness (Titus)

by Phillip Jensen and Tony Payne

Down the centuries, Christians have suffered from the effects of two damaging (and opposite) problems. On the one hand, there always seem to be people wanting to impose rules and regulations for Christians to follow. On the other hand, there have always been Christians who seem not to care about how they live, and who regard God's forgiveness as a blank cheque.

How can we avoid these problems and be motivated to live a life pleasing to God? If the idea of 'being godly' is attractive, how can we turn our vague yearning for it into reality?

In Paul's short letter to Titus, God reveals the path to true godliness. We are warned about false trails and given stirring encouragement about the source of true godliness, its motivation and the shape it will take.

The Path to Godliness contains six Bible studies suitable for group or individual use.